But seek ye first the kingdom of God, and his righteousness; and all these things shall be added unto you. (KJV) *Matthew 6:33*

Date_____

Prayer Type: *Spiritual__ Material__ Physical__*

Prayer Request:
_____
_____
_____
_____
_____
_____
_____
_____
_____
_____

Recent Revelations/Outcomes:
_____
_____
_____
_____
_____
_____
_____
_____
_____
_____
_____
_____
_____
_____

What things must I do or stop doing:
_____
_____
_____
_____
_____
_____
_____
_____

> *But seek ye first the kingdom of God, and his righteousness; and all these things shall be added unto you. (KJV)* Matthew 6:33

Date_____

Prayer Type: *Spiritual__ Material__ Physical__*

Prayer Request:
_____
_____
_____
_____
_____
_____
_____
_____
_____

Recent Revelations/Outcomes:
_____
_____
_____
_____
_____
_____
_____
_____
_____
_____
_____
_____
_____
_____

What things must I do or stop doing:
_____
_____
_____
_____
_____
_____
_____
_____

A PRAYER JOURNAL

"A journal of prayers"

This journal will allow you to keep track of your prayers for your needs. Sometimes we pray for things and forget down the road after they have been answered. This journal will allow you to be thankful for all of those answered prayers while patiently waiting for other prayer request. You can share what God has done for you with your friends, children, and other family members. Establish family prayer requests with your husband and children. Seek God as a family regarding your requests. Grow together in God's blessings.

Be patient and remember; God's time is not our time.

Original copyright of materials ©copyright October 2007.

All rights reserved.

No part of this book may be reproduced without written permission in advance from the publisher except for brief quotes and credits to the publisher.

ISBN 978-0-6151-7571-3

Contact publisher for additional questions or bulk order requests

Angela Claudette Williams

Email Address:

claudetteexpressions@yahoo.com

Website address:

http:www.claudetteexpressions.com

> *But seek ye first the kingdom of God, and his righteousness; and all these things shall be added unto you. (KJV)* Matthew 6:33

Date_____

Prayer Type: *Spiritual__ Material__ Physical__*

Prayer Request:
_____
_____
_____
_____
_____
_____
_____
_____
_____
_____

Recent Revelations/Outcomes:
_____
_____
_____
_____
_____
_____
_____
_____
_____
_____
_____
_____
_____
_____
_____

What things must I do or stop doing:
_____
_____
_____
_____
_____
_____
_____
_____

> ***But seek ye first the kingdom of God, and his righteousness; and all these things shall be added unto you. (KJV)*** *Matthew 6:33*

Date_____

Prayer Type: *Spiritual__ Material__ Physical__*

Prayer Request:
_____
_____
_____
_____
_____
_____
_____
_____
_____

Recent Revelations/Outcomes:
_____
_____
_____
_____
_____
_____
_____
_____
_____
_____
_____
_____
_____
_____
_____

What things must I do or stop doing:
_____
_____
_____
_____
_____
_____
_____
_____

But seek ye first the kingdom of God, and his righteousness; and all these things shall be added unto you. (KJV) *Matthew 6:33*

Date_____

Prayer Type: *Spiritual__ Material__ Physical__*

Prayer Request:
_____
_____
_____
_____
_____
_____
_____
_____
_____

Recent Revelations/Outcomes:
_____
_____
_____
_____
_____
_____
_____
_____
_____
_____
_____
_____
_____
_____

What things must I do or stop doing:
_____
_____
_____
_____
_____
_____
_____
_____

> *But seek ye first the kingdom of God, and his righteousness; and all these things shall be added unto you. (KJV)* Matthew 6:33

Date_____

Prayer Type: *Spiritual__ Material__ Physical__*

Prayer Request:
_____
_____
_____
_____
_____
_____
_____
_____
_____

Recent Revelations/Outcomes:
_____
_____
_____
_____
_____
_____
_____
_____
_____
_____
_____
_____
_____
_____

What things must I do or stop doing:
_____
_____
_____
_____
_____
_____
_____

> ***But seek ye first the kingdom of God, and his righteousness; and all these things shall be added unto you. (KJV)*** *Matthew 6:33*

Date_____

Prayer Type: *Spiritual__ Material__ Physical__*

Prayer Request:
_____
_____
_____
_____
_____
_____
_____
_____
_____

Recent Revelations/Outcomes:
_____
_____
_____
_____
_____
_____
_____
_____
_____
_____
_____
_____
_____
_____

What things must I do or stop doing:
_____
_____
_____
_____
_____
_____
_____
_____

But seek ye first the kingdom of God, and his righteousness; and all these things shall be added unto you. (KJV) Matthew 6:33

Date_____

Prayer Type: *Spiritual___ Material___ Physical___*

Prayer Request:
_____
_____
_____
_____
_____
_____
_____
_____
_____

Recent Revelations/Outcomes:
_____
_____
_____
_____
_____
_____
_____
_____
_____
_____
_____
_____
_____
_____
_____

What things must I do or stop doing:
_____
_____
_____
_____
_____
_____
_____

> ***But seek ye first the kingdom of God, and his righteousness; and all these things shall be added unto you. (KJV)*** *Matthew 6:33*

Date_____

Prayer Type: *Spiritual__ Material__ Physical__*

Prayer Request:
_____
_____
_____
_____
_____
_____
_____
_____

Recent Revelations/Outcomes:
_____
_____
_____
_____
_____
_____
_____
_____
_____
_____
_____
_____
_____

What things must I do or stop doing:
_____
_____
_____
_____
_____
_____
_____

> ***But seek ye first the kingdom of God, and his righteousness; and all these things shall be added unto you. (KJV)*** *Matthew 6:33*

Date_____

Prayer Type: *Spiritual__ Material__ Physical__*

Prayer Request:
_____
_____
_____
_____
_____
_____
_____
_____
_____

Recent Revelations/Outcomes:
_____
_____
_____
_____
_____
_____
_____
_____
_____
_____
_____
_____
_____
_____

What things must I do or stop doing:
_____
_____
_____
_____
_____
_____
_____

But seek ye first the kingdom of God, and his righteousness; and all these things shall be added unto you. (KJV) *Matthew 6:33*

Date_____

Prayer Type: *Spiritual__ Material__ Physical__*

Prayer Request:
_____
_____
_____
_____
_____
_____
_____
_____
_____
_____

Recent Revelations/Outcomes:
_____
_____
_____
_____
_____
_____
_____
_____
_____
_____
_____
_____
_____
_____
_____
_____

What things must I do or stop doing:
_____
_____
_____
_____
_____
_____
_____

But seek ye first the kingdom of God, and his righteousness; and all these things shall be added unto you. (KJV) Matthew 6:33

Date_____

Prayer Type: *Spiritual__ Material__ Physical__*

Prayer Request:
_____
_____
_____
_____
_____
_____
_____
_____
_____

Recent Revelations/Outcomes:
_____
_____
_____
_____
_____
_____
_____
_____
_____
_____
_____
_____
_____
_____
_____

What things must I do or stop doing:
_____
_____
_____
_____
_____
_____
_____

But seek ye first the kingdom of God, and his righteousness; and all these things shall be added unto you. (KJV) Matthew 6:33

Date_____

Prayer Type: *Spiritual__ Material__ Physical__*

Prayer Request:
_____
_____
_____
_____
_____
_____
_____
_____
_____
_____

Recent Revelations/Outcomes:
_____
_____
_____
_____
_____
_____
_____
_____
_____
_____
_____
_____
_____
_____
_____

What things must I do or stop doing:
_____
_____
_____
_____
_____
_____
_____
_____

> ***But seek ye first the kingdom of God, and his righteousness; and all these things shall be added unto you. (KJV)*** *Matthew 6:33*

Date_____

Prayer Type: *Spiritual__ Material__ Physical__*

Prayer Request:
_____
_____
_____
_____
_____
_____
_____
_____
_____
_____
_____

Recent Revelations/Outcomes:
_____
_____
_____
_____
_____
_____
_____
_____
_____
_____
_____
_____
_____
_____
_____

What things must I do or stop doing:
_____
_____
_____
_____
_____
_____
_____
_____

> ***But seek ye first the kingdom of God, and his righteousness; and all these things shall be added unto you. (KJV)*** *Matthew 6:33*

Date_____

Prayer Type: *Spiritual__ Material__ Physical__*

Prayer Request:
_____
_____
_____
_____
_____
_____
_____
_____
_____

Recent Revelations/Outcomes:
_____
_____
_____
_____
_____
_____
_____
_____
_____
_____
_____
_____
_____
_____
_____

What things must I do or stop doing:
_____
_____
_____
_____
_____
_____
_____
_____

> **But seek ye first the kingdom of God, and his righteousness; and all these things shall be added unto you. (KJV)** *Matthew 6:33*

Date_____

Prayer Type: *Spiritual__ Material__ Physical__*

Prayer Request:
_____
_____
_____
_____
_____
_____
_____
_____
_____

Recent Revelations/Outcomes:
_____
_____
_____
_____
_____
_____
_____
_____
_____
_____
_____
_____
_____

What things must I do or stop doing:
_____
_____
_____
_____
_____
_____
_____

> ***But seek ye first the kingdom of God, and his righteousness; and all these things shall be added unto you. (KJV)*** *Matthew 6:33*

Date_____

Prayer Type: *Spiritual__ Material__ Physical__*

Prayer Request:
_____
_____
_____
_____
_____
_____
_____
_____
_____
_____

Recent Revelations/Outcomes:
_____
_____
_____
_____
_____
_____
_____
_____
_____
_____
_____
_____
_____
_____
_____

What things must I do or stop doing:
_____
_____
_____
_____
_____
_____
_____

But seek ye first the kingdom of God, and his righteousness; and all these things shall be added unto you. (KJV) Matthew 6:33

Date_____

Prayer Type: *Spiritual__ Material__ Physical__*

Prayer Request:
_____
_____
_____
_____
_____
_____
_____
_____

Recent Revelations/Outcomes:
_____
_____
_____
_____
_____
_____
_____
_____
_____
_____
_____
_____
_____
_____

What things must I do or stop doing:
_____
_____
_____
_____
_____
_____
_____

> *But seek ye first the kingdom of God, and his righteousness; and all these things shall be added unto you. (KJV)* Matthew 6:33

Date_____

Prayer Type: *Spiritual__ Material__ Physical__*

Prayer Request:
_____
_____
_____
_____
_____
_____
_____
_____
_____
_____

Recent Revelations/Outcomes:
_____
_____
_____
_____
_____
_____
_____
_____
_____
_____
_____
_____
_____
_____
_____

What things must I do or stop doing:
_____
_____
_____
_____
_____
_____
_____
_____

> **But seek ye first the kingdom of God, and his righteousness; and all these things shall be added unto you. (KJV)** *Matthew 6:33*

Date_____

Prayer Type: *Spiritual__ Material__ Physical__*

Prayer Request:
_____
_____
_____
_____
_____
_____
_____
_____
_____

Recent Revelations/Outcomes:
_____
_____
_____
_____
_____
_____
_____
_____
_____
_____
_____
_____
_____

What things must I do or stop doing:
_____
_____
_____
_____
_____
_____
_____

> ***But seek ye first the kingdom of God, and his righteousness; and all these things shall be added unto you. (KJV)*** *Matthew 6:33*

Date_____

Prayer Type: *Spiritual__ Material__ Physical__*

Prayer Request:

_____
_____
_____
_____
_____
_____
_____
_____
_____

Recent Revelations/Outcomes:

_____
_____
_____
_____
_____
_____
_____
_____
_____
_____
_____
_____
_____
_____
_____

What things must I do or stop doing:

_____
_____
_____
_____
_____
_____
_____
_____
_____

> ***But seek ye first the kingdom of God, and his righteousness; and all these things shall be added unto you. (KJV)*** *Matthew 6:33*

Date_____

Prayer Type: *Spiritual__ Material__ Physical__*

Prayer Request:
_____
_____
_____
_____
_____
_____
_____
_____

Recent Revelations/Outcomes:
_____
_____
_____
_____
_____
_____
_____
_____
_____
_____
_____
_____
_____

What things must I do or stop doing:
_____
_____
_____
_____
_____
_____
_____

But seek ye first the kingdom of God, and his righteousness; and all these things shall be added unto you. (KJV) *Matthew 6:33*

Date_____

Prayer Type: *Spiritual__ Material__ Physical__*

Prayer Request:
_____
_____
_____
_____
_____
_____
_____
_____
_____

Recent Revelations/Outcomes:
_____
_____
_____
_____
_____
_____
_____
_____
_____
_____
_____
_____
_____
_____

What things must I do or stop doing:
_____
_____
_____
_____
_____
_____
_____

> **But seek ye first the kingdom of God, and his righteousness; and all these things shall be added unto you. (KJV)** Matthew 6:33

Date_____

Prayer Type: *Spiritual__ Material__ Physical__*

Prayer Request:
_____
_____
_____
_____
_____
_____
_____
_____
_____

Recent Revelations/Outcomes:
_____
_____
_____
_____
_____
_____
_____
_____
_____
_____
_____
_____
_____
_____

What things must I do or stop doing:
_____
_____
_____
_____
_____
_____
_____

> *But seek ye first the kingdom of God, and his righteousness; and all these things shall be added unto you. (KJV)* Matthew 6:33

Date_____

Prayer Type: *Spiritual__ Material__ Physical__*

Prayer Request:
_____
_____
_____
_____
_____
_____
_____
_____
_____
_____

Recent Revelations/Outcomes:
_____
_____
_____
_____
_____
_____
_____
_____
_____
_____
_____
_____
_____
_____
_____
_____

What things must I do or stop doing:
_____
_____
_____
_____
_____
_____
_____
_____

But seek ye first the kingdom of God, and his righteousness; and all these things shall be added unto you. (KJV) Matthew 6:33

Date_____

Prayer Type: *Spiritual__ Material__ Physical__*

Prayer Request:
_____
_____
_____
_____
_____
_____
_____
_____
_____

Recent Revelations/Outcomes:
_____
_____
_____
_____
_____
_____
_____
_____
_____
_____
_____
_____
_____
_____
_____

What things must I do or stop doing:
_____
_____
_____
_____
_____
_____
_____

> **But seek ye first the kingdom of God, and his righteousness; and all these things shall be added unto you. (KJV)** *Matthew 6:33*

Date_____

Prayer Type: *Spiritual__ Material__ Physical__*

Prayer Request:
_____
_____
_____
_____
_____
_____
_____
_____
_____

Recent Revelations/Outcomes:
_____
_____
_____
_____
_____
_____
_____
_____
_____
_____
_____
_____
_____
_____

What things must I do or stop doing:
_____
_____
_____
_____
_____
_____
_____

> **But seek ye first the kingdom of God, and his righteousness; and all these things shall be added unto you. (KJV)** *Matthew 6:33*

Date_____

Prayer Type: *Spiritual__ Material__ Physical__*

Prayer Request:
_____
_____
_____
_____
_____
_____
_____
_____
_____
_____

Recent Revelations/Outcomes:
_____
_____
_____
_____
_____
_____
_____
_____
_____
_____
_____
_____
_____
_____
_____
_____

What things must I do or stop doing:
_____
_____
_____
_____
_____
_____
_____
_____

> ***But seek ye first the kingdom of God, and his righteousness; and all these things shall be added unto you. (KJV)*** *Matthew 6:33*

Date_____

Prayer Type: *Spiritual__ Material__ Physical__*

Prayer Request:
_____
_____
_____
_____
_____
_____
_____
_____

Recent Revelations/Outcomes:
_____
_____
_____
_____
_____
_____
_____
_____
_____
_____
_____
_____
_____

What things must I do or stop doing:
_____
_____
_____
_____
_____
_____
_____

> ***But seek ye first the kingdom of God, and his righteousness; and all these things shall be added unto you. (KJV)*** *Matthew 6:33*

Date_____

Prayer Type: *Spiritual__ Material__ Physical__*

Prayer Request:
_____
_____
_____
_____
_____
_____
_____
_____

Recent Revelations/Outcomes:
_____
_____
_____
_____
_____
_____
_____
_____
_____
_____
_____
_____
_____
_____

What things must I do or stop doing:
_____
_____
_____
_____
_____
_____
_____

> **But seek ye first the kingdom of God, and his righteousness; and all these things shall be added unto you. (KJV)** *Matthew 6:33*

Date_____

Prayer Type: *Spiritual__ Material__ Physical__*

Prayer Request:
_____
_____
_____
_____
_____
_____
_____
_____
_____
_____

Recent Revelations/Outcomes:
_____
_____
_____
_____
_____
_____
_____
_____
_____
_____
_____
_____
_____
_____
_____

What things must I do or stop doing:
_____
_____
_____
_____
_____
_____
_____
_____

> *But seek ye first the kingdom of God, and his righteousness; and all these things shall be added unto you. (KJV)* Matthew 6:33

Date_____

Prayer Type: *Spiritual__ Material__ Physical__*

Prayer Request:
_____
_____
_____
_____
_____
_____
_____
_____
_____
_____

Recent Revelations/Outcomes:
_____
_____
_____
_____
_____
_____
_____
_____
_____
_____
_____
_____
_____
_____
_____

What things must I do or stop doing:
_____
_____
_____
_____
_____
_____
_____
_____

> ***But seek ye first the kingdom of God, and his righteousness; and all these things shall be added unto you. (KJV)*** *Matthew 6:33*

Date_____

Prayer Type: *Spiritual__ Material__ Physical__*

Prayer Request:
_____
_____
_____
_____
_____
_____
_____
_____
_____
_____

Recent Revelations/Outcomes:
_____
_____
_____
_____
_____
_____
_____
_____
_____
_____
_____
_____
_____
_____
_____

What things must I do or stop doing:
_____
_____
_____
_____
_____
_____
_____
_____

> ***But seek ye first the kingdom of God, and his righteousness; and all these things shall be added unto you. (KJV)*** *Matthew 6:33*

Date_____

Prayer Type: *Spiritual__ Material__ Physical__*

Prayer Request:
_____
_____
_____
_____
_____
_____
_____
_____
_____

Recent Revelations/Outcomes:
_____
_____
_____
_____
_____
_____
_____
_____
_____
_____
_____
_____
_____
_____
_____

What things must I do or stop doing:
_____
_____
_____
_____
_____
_____
_____
_____

But seek ye first the kingdom of God, and his righteousness; and all these things shall be added unto you. (KJV) *Matthew 6:33*

Date_____

Prayer Type: *Spiritual__ Material__ Physical__*

Prayer Request:
_____
_____
_____
_____
_____
_____
_____
_____

Recent Revelations/Outcomes:
_____
_____
_____
_____
_____
_____
_____
_____
_____
_____
_____
_____
_____
_____

What things must I do or stop doing:
_____
_____
_____
_____
_____
_____
_____

> *But seek ye first the kingdom of God, and his righteousness; and all these things shall be added unto you. (KJV)* Matthew 6:33

Date_____

Prayer Type: *Spiritual__ Material__ Physical__*

Prayer Request:
_____
_____
_____
_____
_____
_____
_____
_____

Recent Revelations/Outcomes:
_____
_____
_____
_____
_____
_____
_____
_____
_____
_____
_____
_____
_____

What things must I do or stop doing:
_____
_____
_____
_____
_____
_____
_____

But seek ye first the kingdom of God, and his righteousness; and all these things shall be added unto you. (KJV) Matthew 6:33

Date_____

Prayer Type: *Spiritual__ Material__ Physical__*

Prayer Request:
_____
_____
_____
_____
_____
_____
_____
_____
_____
_____

Recent Revelations/Outcomes:
_____
_____
_____
_____
_____
_____
_____
_____
_____
_____
_____
_____
_____
_____
_____

What things must I do or stop doing:
_____
_____
_____
_____
_____
_____
_____

> *But seek ye first the kingdom of God, and his righteousness; and all these things shall be added unto you. (KJV)* Matthew 6:33

Date_____

Prayer Type: *Spiritual__ Material__ Physical__*

Prayer Request:
_____
_____
_____
_____
_____
_____
_____
_____

Recent Revelations/Outcomes:
_____
_____
_____
_____
_____
_____
_____
_____
_____
_____
_____
_____
_____
_____

What things must I do or stop doing:
_____
_____
_____
_____
_____
_____
_____
_____

> *But seek ye first the kingdom of God, and his righteousness; and all these things shall be added unto you. (KJV)* Matthew 6:33

Date_____

Prayer Type: *Spiritual__ Material__ Physical__*

Prayer Request:
_____
_____
_____
_____
_____
_____
_____
_____
_____
_____

Recent Revelations/Outcomes:
_____
_____
_____
_____
_____
_____
_____
_____
_____
_____
_____
_____
_____
_____

What things must I do or stop doing:
_____
_____
_____
_____
_____
_____
_____
_____

> *But seek ye first the kingdom of God, and his righteousness; and all these things shall be added unto you. (KJV)* Matthew 6:33

Date_____

Prayer Type: *Spiritual__ Material__ Physical__*

Prayer Request:
_____
_____
_____
_____
_____
_____
_____
_____
_____

Recent Revelations/Outcomes:
_____
_____
_____
_____
_____
_____
_____
_____
_____
_____
_____
_____
_____
_____
_____
_____

What things must I do or stop doing:
_____
_____
_____
_____
_____
_____
_____
_____

But seek ye first the kingdom of God, and his righteousness; and all these things shall be added unto you. (KJV) *Matthew 6:33*

Date_____

Prayer Type: *Spiritual__ Material__ Physical__*

Prayer Request:
_____
_____
_____
_____
_____
_____
_____
_____
_____

Recent Revelations/Outcomes:
_____
_____
_____
_____
_____
_____
_____
_____
_____
_____
_____
_____
_____
_____

What things must I do or stop doing:
_____
_____
_____
_____
_____
_____
_____

But seek ye first the kingdom of God, and his righteousness; and all these things shall be added unto you. (KJV) Matthew 6:33

Date_____

Prayer Type: *Spiritual__ Material__ Physical__*

Prayer Request:
_____
_____
_____
_____
_____
_____
_____
_____

Recent Revelations/Outcomes:
_____
_____
_____
_____
_____
_____
_____
_____
_____
_____
_____
_____
_____

What things must I do or stop doing:
_____
_____
_____
_____
_____
_____
_____

> ***But seek ye first the kingdom of God, and his righteousness; and all these things shall be added unto you. (KJV)*** *Matthew 6:33*

Date_____

Prayer Type: *Spiritual__ Material__ Physical__*

Prayer Request:
_____
_____
_____
_____
_____
_____
_____
_____
_____
_____

Recent Revelations/Outcomes:
_____
_____
_____
_____
_____
_____
_____
_____
_____
_____
_____
_____
_____
_____
_____

What things must I do or stop doing:
_____
_____
_____
_____
_____
_____
_____

> *But seek ye first the kingdom of God, and his righteousness; and all these things shall be added unto you. (KJV)* Matthew 6:33

Date_____

Prayer Type: *Spiritual__ Material__ Physical__*

Prayer Request:
_____
_____
_____
_____
_____
_____
_____
_____
_____

Recent Revelations/Outcomes:
_____
_____
_____
_____
_____
_____
_____
_____
_____
_____
_____
_____
_____
_____
_____

What things must I do or stop doing:
_____
_____
_____
_____
_____
_____
_____

> ***But seek ye first the kingdom of God, and his righteousness; and all these things shall be added unto you. (KJV)*** *Matthew 6:33*

Date_____

Prayer Type: *Spiritual__ Material__ Physical__*

Prayer Request:
_____
_____
_____
_____
_____
_____
_____
_____
_____
_____

Recent Revelations/Outcomes:
_____
_____
_____
_____
_____
_____
_____
_____
_____
_____
_____
_____
_____
_____
_____

What things must I do or stop doing:
_____
_____
_____
_____
_____
_____
_____

But seek ye first the kingdom of God, and his righteousness; and all these things shall be added unto you. (KJV) Matthew 6:33

Date_____

Prayer Type: *Spiritual__ Material__ Physical__*

Prayer Request:
_____
_____
_____
_____
_____
_____
_____
_____
_____

Recent Revelations/Outcomes:
_____
_____
_____
_____
_____
_____
_____
_____
_____
_____
_____
_____
_____
_____
_____
_____

What things must I do or stop doing:
_____
_____
_____
_____
_____
_____
_____
_____

> *But seek ye first the kingdom of God, and his righteousness; and all these things shall be added unto you. (KJV)* Matthew 6:33

Date_____

Prayer Type: *Spiritual__ Material__ Physical__*

Prayer Request:
_____
_____
_____
_____
_____
_____
_____
_____
_____

Recent Revelations/Outcomes:
_____
_____
_____
_____
_____
_____
_____
_____
_____
_____
_____
_____
_____
_____
_____

What things must I do or stop doing:
_____
_____
_____
_____
_____
_____
_____

> *But seek ye first the kingdom of God, and his righteousness; and all these things shall be added unto you. (KJV)* Matthew 6:33

Date_____

Prayer Type: *Spiritual__ Material__ Physical__*

Prayer Request:
_____
_____
_____
_____
_____
_____
_____
_____
_____

Recent Revelations/Outcomes:
_____
_____
_____
_____
_____
_____
_____
_____
_____
_____
_____
_____
_____
_____
_____

What things must I do or stop doing:
_____
_____
_____
_____
_____
_____
_____
_____

www.ingramcontent.com/pod-product-compliance
Lightning Source LLC
Chambersburg PA
CBHW051718040426

42446CB00008B/951